Maya Angelou Biography for Kids

The Inspiring Journey From a Mute Girl to a World-Famous Poet, Championing Freedom, Traveling the World, and Leaving a Lasting Legacy for New Readers

Academic Press

Copyright © 2024 by Academic Press

All rights reserved. No part of this publication may be reproduced, distributed, or transmitted in any form or by any means, including photocopying, recording, or other electronic or mechanical methods, without the prior written permission of the publisher, except in the case of brief quotations embodied in critical reviews and certain other noncommercial uses permitted by copyright law. For permission requests, write to the publisher at [academicpresss@outlook.com].

Table of contents

1. Introduction
2. Early Years
   - Birth and childhood
   - Challenges faced as a mute girl
3. Finding Her Voice
   - Discovering her love for literature and writing
   - Overcoming speech impediment
4. Rising Above Adversity
   - Difficulties during her early years
   - Resilience and determinations
5. Becoming a World-Famous Poet
   - Exploration of Maya Angelou's poetic journey
   - Notable works and their impact
6. Championing Freedom
   - Involvement in the Civil Rights Movement
   - Advocacy for equality and justice
7. Traveling the World
   - Maya Angelou's global experiences
   - Cultural influences on her work
8. Leaving a Lasting Legacy
   - Impact on literature and society
   - Recognition and honors received

9. Maya Angelou's Wisdom
- Inspirational quotes and life lessons for kids
- Reflection on her teachings
10. Fun Facts and Trivia
- Engaging tidbits about Maya Angelou's life
- Interesting anecdotes for young readers
11. Timeline of Maya Angelou's Life
- Chronological overview from birth to legacy
12. Activities and Exercises
- Interactive content to engage young readers
- Creative projects inspired by Maya Angelou's life
13. Conclusion

1. Introduction

Have you ever seen a bird take flight with words instead of wings? A bird whose voice could break open silence and mend hearts with poetry? Maya Angelou was that kind of bird. She lived a life so vibrant, so rich, that you could fill a whole library with its stories. But where do you even begin with a life like hers? Well, let's start with a little riddle...

She was born silent, yet her voice shook the world.
She faced darkness, yet wrote poems bathed in sunshine.
She knew pain, yet taught others the melody of resilience.

Who was this woman, this talking bird whose words soared the sky? Open this book, and let Maya Angelou herself answer the riddle.

2. Early Years
- Birth and childhood

Maya Angelou was born on a stormy night in April, 1928. Her parents named her Marguerite Johnson, but her brother Bailey called her Maya, which means "my sister" in Spanish. Maya's parents were young and restless. They wanted to pursue their dreams of being a nurse and a sailor, but they had to take care of two children. They often argued and fought, and sometimes they left Maya and Bailey alone for days.

When Maya was three years old, her parents decided to end their marriage. They sent Maya and Bailey on a train to Stamps, Arkansas, where their grandmother, Momma, lived. Momma owned a general store that sold everything from candy to cotton. She was a strong and religious woman who taught Maya and Bailey about God, manners, and hard work. She also protected them from the dangers of racism and segregation that were common in the South.

Maya loved living with Momma and Bailey. She enjoyed reading books, playing games, and listening to stories. She also liked to explore the nature around her. She was fascinated by the birds, flowers, and trees. She felt a connection with them, as if they were her friends. She often imagined that she could fly like a bird, or grow like a flower, or stand tall like a tree.

But Maya's life was not always happy and peaceful. She also faced many challenges and hardships. She was bullied by some of the white kids at school, who called her names and threw rocks at her. She was confused by the rules and customs that separated black and white people, such as drinking from different fountains, sitting in different seats, and using different bathrooms. She was hurt by some of the people she trusted, such as her father, who abandoned her again, and her mother's boyfriend, who abused her.

One of the most traumatic events in Maya's childhood was when she was raped by her mother's boyfriend when she was eight years old. She was so scared and ashamed that she told only Bailey what had happened. Bailey told their mother, who called the police. The man was arrested, but he was released after a few days. He was later found dead, probably killed by some of Maya's relatives.

Maya felt that her words had caused the man's death. She thought that God was angry with her for telling the truth. She decided to stop talking to anyone except Bailey. She became mute for five years. She thought that by being silent, she could avoid hurting anyone else.

But Maya did not stop loving words. She continued to read books and poems, and to write her own thoughts and feelings in a diary. She also found comfort and support from some of the people in her life, such as Momma, who prayed for her, and Mrs. Flowers, a kind and educated woman who encouraged her to read aloud and appreciate the beauty of language.

Slowly, Maya began to heal and to speak again. She realized that her words had power, not only to harm, but also to heal, to express, and to inspire. She decided to use her words to tell her story and to celebrate her identity as a black woman. She changed her name to Maya Angelou, which combined her childhood nickname and her first husband's surname. She embarked on a journey of discovery and adventure that would take her to many places and roles. She became a writer, a poet, a dancer, a singer, a actress, a teacher, and an activist. She became a phenomenal woman.```

- Challenges faced as a mute girl

Imagine that you have something important to say, but you can't say it. Imagine that you have a question, a joke, a compliment, or a complaint, but you can't express it. Imagine that you have a voice, but you can't use it. How would you feel?

This is how Maya Angelou felt for five years of her life. She was a mute girl, a girl who could not speak. She was not born mute, but she became mute after a terrible thing happened to her. She was raped by her mother's boyfriend when she was eight years old. She was so scared and ashamed that she told only her brother Bailey what had happened. Bailey told their mother, who called the police. The man was arrested, but he was released after a few days.

He was later found dead, probably killed by some of Maya's relatives.

Maya felt that her words had caused the man's death. She thought that God was angry with her for telling the truth. She decided to stop talking to anyone except Bailey. She became mute for five years. She thought that by being silent, she could avoid hurting anyone else.

But being silent was not easy. Maya faced many challenges and hardships as a mute girl. She had to communicate with gestures, nods, and shakes of her head. She had to write notes or point at things to make herself understood. She had to endure the teasing and taunting of some of the kids at school, who called her dumb, crazy, or weird. She had to cope with the frustration and loneliness of not being able to share her thoughts and feelings with anyone.

But Maya also had moments of resilience and hope. She had her brother Bailey, who was her best friend and protector. He understood her without words, and he always stood up for her. He also gave her books and poems to read, which opened her mind to new worlds and possibilities. He also gave her a nickname, Maya, which means "my sister" in Spanish.

She had her grandmother Momma, who was her guardian and mentor. She taught her about God, manners, and hard work. She also prayed for her every day, and she never gave up on her. She also gave her a safe and loving home, where she could feel comfortable and secure.

She had Mrs. Flowers, who was her teacher and inspiration. She encouraged her to read aloud and appreciate the beauty of language. She also gave her cookies and lemonade, and she treated her with respect and kindness. She also gave her a gift, a gift that changed her life. She gave her a book of poetry by Paul Laurence Dunbar, a black poet who wrote about the joys and sorrows of his people.

One day, Maya was reading one of Dunbar's poems, called "Sympathy". It was about a caged bird that sings of freedom. Maya felt a connection with the bird, and with the poet. She felt that they understood her pain and her longing. She felt that they spoke for her, and to her. She felt a stir in her heart, and a tickle in her throat. She felt a word forming in her mouth, and she let it out. She said the word "poetry".

It was the first word she had spoken in five years. It was the word that broke her silence. It was the word that gave her back her voice.

Maya was overjoyed and amazed. She realized that her words had power, not only to harm, but also to heal, to express, and to inspire. She decided to use her words to tell her story and to celebrate her identity as a black woman. She changed her name to Maya Angelou, which combined her childhood nickname and her first husband's surname. She embarked on a journey of discovery and adventure that would take her to many places and roles. She became a writer, a poet, a dancer, a singer, a actress, a teacher, and an activist. She became a phenomenal woman.

3. Finding Her Voice

- Discovering her love for literature and writing

Maya Angelou loved words. She loved how they sounded, how they felt, how they made her think. She loved to read books, to listen to stories, to write poems. She loved to learn new things, to explore new places, to meet new people.

But Maya Angelou did not always love words. When she was a little girl, after the death of her rapist that made her stop talking, She was sent to live with her grandmother in a small town in Arkansas, where she faced racism and discrimination. She felt lonely and afraid, and she thought that her words had no power.

One day, a kind lady named Mrs. Flowers came to visit her. She was a friend of Maya's grandmother, and she was a teacher and a reader. She invited Maya to her home, where she had a library full of books. She gave Maya a book by Charles Dickens, and told her to read it aloud. She said,

"Words mean more than what is set down on paper. It takes the human voice to infuse them with deeper meaning."

Maya was shy and scared, but she was also curious and eager. She opened the book, and began to read. She felt the words come alive in her mouth, in her ears, in her heart. She felt a connection with the characters, with the author, with Mrs. Flowers. She felt a spark of joy, of hope, of freedom.

That was the moment that Maya Angelou discovered her love for literature and writing. She realized that words had power, that they could heal, inspire, and transform. She decided to speak again, and to share her voice with the world. She became a writer and a poet, a storyteller and a teacher, a leader and a activist. She wrote about her life, her struggles, her dreams, and her triumphs. She wrote for herself, and for others. She wrote to celebrate the beauty and the resilience of the human spirit.

- Overcoming speech impediment

Maya was a quiet girl. She had not spoken a word for five years. She was afraid that her words could hurt people, or make them go away. She had lost her parents, her brother, and her uncle. She had been hurt by a man who should have protected her. She had seen the ugliness of racism and violence. She had no voice, and no hope.

But Maya had a gift. She had a memory that could store words like treasures. She had read every book in the library of her small town in Arkansas. She had learned from great writers like Shakespeare, Poe, and Dunbar. She had listened to the stories of her grandmother, her friends, and her community. She had a mind that could imagine worlds beyond her own.

One day, a woman named Mrs. Flowers came into her life. She was a teacher, a reader, and a friend. She saw the potential in Maya, and she wanted to help her find her voice. She gave her books to read, and asked her questions to answer. She encouraged her to write her thoughts, feelings, and dreams. She taught her that words had power, and that she had power too.

Maya was curious, and eager. She wanted to learn more, to express more, to be more. She opened the books, and read them aloud. She felt the words come alive in her mouth, in her ears, in her heart. She felt a connection with the characters, with the authors, with Mrs. Flowers. She felt a spark of joy, of hope, of freedom.

That was the beginning of Maya's triumphant journey. She decided to speak again, and to share her voice with the world. She faced many challenges, but she never gave up. She became a writer, a poet, a storyteller, a teacher, a leader, and an activist. She wrote about her life, her struggles, her dreams, and her triumphs. She wrote for herself, and for others. She wrote to inspire, to empower, and to transform. She wrote to show the beauty and the resilience of the human spirit.

4. Rising Above Adversity
- *Difficulties during her early years*

Maya was a lonely girl. She had no home, no parents, no voice. She had only her brother, Bailey, who loved her and protected her. They were sent from one place to another, never staying long enough to make friends or feel safe. They lived with their grandmother in a small town in Arkansas, where they faced racism and discrimination every day. They lived with their mother in St. Louis, where they faced violence and abuse. They lived with their father in California, where they faced neglect and danger.

Maya was a hurt girl. She had been raped by her mother's boyfriend when she was eight years old. She had told the truth, and he had been killed. She had blamed herself, and stopped talking. She had felt dirty, and ashamed. She had felt guilty, and afraid. She had felt powerless, and hopeless.

Maya was a brave girl. She had not given up on herself, or on life. She had found comfort in books, and in stories. She had found strength in her brother, and in her grandmother.

She had found courage in her teachers, and in her friends. She had found healing in her words, and in her voice.

Maya was a resilient girl. She had overcome many difficulties, and faced many challenges. She had learned from her mistakes, and from her successes. She had grown from her pain, and from her joy. She had transformed from a victim, to a survivor. She had become a writer, a poet, a storyteller, a teacher, a leader, and an activist. She had become Maya Angelou.

- Resilience and determinations

Imagine a young girl named Maya, barely seven years old, thrust into a world shrouded in silence. A world where cruel words stole her voice, leaving her trapped in a cage of her own making. Yet, within this cage, a spark flickered. A spark of resilience, ignited by the embers of Maya's undying spirit.

Life wasn't kind to Maya. Racism's sting was a constant thrumming bassline, poverty played a mournful melody, and the trauma of abuse felt like a discordant harmony that threatened to consume her. But Maya danced a defiant counterpoint. She found solace in books, their words weaving a tapestry of hope across the bare canvases of her days. Each page whispered forgotten dreams awake, urging her to reclaim her voice.

With unwavering determination, Maya began to write. Her pen, dipped in the ink of resilience, scratched out stories of hardship and triumph, of pain and perseverance. In each word, she wrestled back her stolen voice, transforming her silence into a symphony of resistance.

Education became her shield, each lesson a brick in the fortress of her self-belief. Though faced with discrimination and prejudice, Maya refused to cower. She stood tall, her voice ringing clear in classrooms and on stages, challenging injustices with the grace of a ballerina and the power of a lioness.

But the path to her dreams wasn't paved with roses. It was a treacherous climb, riddled with thorns of doubt and despair. There were moments when the weight of oppression threatened to crush her spirit, when the whispers of defeat clawed at her resolve. Yet, Maya pressed on, fueled by an unwavering belief in herself and the inherent worth of every human being.

Her resilience blossomed into action. She marched alongside giants of the Civil Rights Movement, her voice joining the chorus of freedom, each step a testament to her unwavering determination. She became a beacon of hope for the downtrodden, a fierce advocate for equality, using her words as weapons against discrimination and injustice.

And throughout it all, Maya never forgot the power of love. Love for her family, her community, and for the human spirit itself. This love was the balm that soothed her wounds, the fuel that propelled her forward, the melody that harmonized with her resilience.

Maya Angelou's story is an anthem of human strength, a testament to the unyielding power of resilience. It's a story that whispers to every young heart, "No matter the thorns that prick your path, no matter the storms that rage around you, dance through them with unwavering determination.

Let your voice rise above the din, let your spirit soar on wings of hope, and remember, even the smallest bird can leave the mightiest footprints in the sands of time."

So, dear reader, draw inspiration from Maya's unwavering spirit. Let her story be your compass, guiding you through life's storms. Face your challenges with her strength, embrace your struggles with her grace, and let your own resilience bloom into a testament to the human spirit's boundless potential. For within you, too, lies the power to dance through thorns and leave the world a little brighter, a little braver, and a whole lot more hopeful.

5. Becoming a World-Famous Poet

- Exploration of Maya Angelou's poetic journey

Life's storms tossed Maya, scattering her dreams like autumn leaves. Yet, in the cracks of hardship, something extraordinary bloomed. Books became her refuge, their words the wind beneath her clipped wings. Maya devoured them whole, from Shakespeare's sonnets to Harlem Renaissance rhythms, each poem a stepping stone on her path to becoming a poet.

Paul Robeson, a giant of a man with a voice that rumbled like thunder, became her mentor. He showed her the power of poetry to heal, to fight, to sing the unsung stories of her people. Maya, then, started weaving her own tapestries of words. She painted with bluesy brushstrokes, her poems echoing the struggles and triumphs of Black America.

One sweltering Mississippi summer, a spark ignited. Maya, mute for five years after a brutal trauma, found her voice again. It poured out in rhythmic whispers, then roars, giving birth to "I Know Why the Caged Bird Sings" – a raw, unflinching tale of her childhood's darkness, laced with threads of hope and resilience. This book, her song of freedom, shattered silence and resonated with readers across the globe.

But Maya's journey wasn't just about pain. She danced with joy, too, celebrating beauty in "Phenomenal Woman," where her words spun a shimmering cloak of self-love for all to wear. She sang of resilience in "Still I Rise," her voice, a defiant melody soaring above the hate, whispering "I'll rise like dust I'll rise in spite of the lies."

And then there was "On the Pulse of Morning," a poem woven from threads of hope and unity, penned for President Clinton's inauguration. Maya's words, dipped in moonlight and dawn's promise, painted a vision of a nation healed, where "hope rises like yeast."

Through it all, Maya's creative process was a beautiful dance. Sometimes, poems erupted like wildfires, consuming her in a fever of creation. Other times, they simmered like stews, words marinating in life's experiences until they were ready to spill onto the page. She found inspiration everywhere – in the sway of a willow tree, the clatter of a train, the crinkled eyes of an old woman.

For Maya, poetry wasn't just a string of words; it was a bridge, connecting hearts across oceans and generations. It was a mirror, reflecting the beauty and pain of the human experience. It was a weapon, fighting for justice and equality. And it was a song, weaving tales of hope and love that transcended the boundaries of time and space.

- Notable works and their impact

She wrote about her life and the world around her, using her words to inspire and empower others. She was one of the most influential voices in American literature and culture, and her works have a lasting impact on readers of all ages and backgrounds.

Y KK jfMaya Angelou's notable works are:

- I Know Why the Caged Bird Sings: This is the first of her seven autobiographies, and it tells the story of her childhood and adolescence in the segregated South. She faced racism, poverty, violence, and abuse, but she also found strength, joy, and beauty in her family, friends, and books. She learned to overcome her fears and challenges, and to express herself through writing and speaking. This book is a classic of American literature, and it opened up new ways of talking about race, gender, and trauma.

- Just Give Me a Cool Drink of Water 'fore I Diiie: This is her first collection of poetry, and it showcases her skill and diversity as a poet. She writes about love, pain, hope, and humor, using vivid imagery, musical language, and powerful emotions. She also explores the themes of identity, culture, and history, especially from the perspective of Black women. This book was nominated for the Pulitzer Prize, and it established her as a prominent poet.

- On the Pulse of Morning: This is the poem that she recited at the inauguration of President Bill Clinton in 1993. She was the first poet to do so since Robert Frost in 1961, and the first African-American and woman to do so. She addressed the nation and the world, calling for peace, unity, and responsibility. She also celebrated the diversity and potential of humanity, and the beauty and fragility of nature. She urged everyone to wake up and face the new day with courage and hope. This poem was a historic and inspiring moment, and it was later published as a book.

- Phenomenal Woman: This is one of her most popular and beloved poems, and it is part of her collection And Still I Rise. It is a poem of self-love and confidence, in which she celebrates her beauty, strength, and grace as a woman. She rejects the stereotypes and expectations of society, and embraces her own uniqueness and worth. She also encourages other women to do the same, and to be proud of who they are. This poem is a feminist anthem, and it has been recited and shared by many women around the world.

Maya Angelou's works had a profound impact on literature and society, because they:

- Challenged the norms and conventions of writing, and created new forms and styles of expression.
- Reflected the realities and experiences of marginalized groups, especially Black women, and gave them a voice and a platform.

- Addressed the issues and problems of the times, such as racism, sexism, violence, and injustice, and advocated for change and action.

- Inspired and influenced many other writers and artists, both in the US and abroad, who followed her example and vision.

- Educated and enlightened many readers and audiences, who learned from her wisdom and insights, and connected with her stories and emotions.

- Motivated and empowered many people, especially women and people of color, who found hope and courage in her words, and followed their dreams and passions.

Maya Angelou's words have a lasting influence on the world, because they:

- Continue to resonate and speak to the current and future generations, who face similar or new challenges and opportunities.

- Continue to spark curiosity and appreciation for the art and power of storytelling, poetry, and language.

- Continue to create a legacy and a community of people who share her values and ideals, and who strive to make the world a better place.

6. Championing Freedom

- *Involvement in the Civil Rights Movement*

Maya Angelou was a woman of courage and conviction. She was not only a writer, a poet, an actress, and a teacher, but also an activist who fought for the rights and dignity of all people. She was deeply involved in the Civil Rights Movement, a struggle to end racial discrimination and segregation in the United States.

Maya Angelou's involvement in the Civil Rights Movement began in the late 1950s, when she met and befriended some of the most influential leaders and figures of the movement. She was inspired by Martin Luther King Jr., the charismatic preacher and organizer who led the Southern Christian Leadership Conference (SCLC), a group that coordinated nonviolent protests and campaigns for civil rights. She was also influenced by Malcolm X, the fiery speaker and activist who advocated for Black nationalism and self-defense. She was close to James Baldwin, the brilliant writer and critic who exposed the realities and complexities of racism in America. She was also connected to many other activists, artists, and organizations that worked for social justice and human rights.

Maya Angelou's involvement in the Civil Rights Movement took many forms and shapes. She was a fundraiser, a coordinator, a speaker, a writer, and a participant in various events and actions. She organized a cabaret for freedom to raise money for the SCLC in 1959[^1^][1]. She served as the northern coordinator for the SCLC in 1960[^1^][1]. She joined Malcolm X in planning for an Organization of Afro-American Unity in 1964[^2^][2]. She marched with Gloria Steinem and other women in the Women's Strike for Equality in 1970[^3^][3]. She recited her poem "On the Pulse of Morning" at the inauguration of President Bill Clinton in 1993. She also supported many other causes and movements, such as the anti-apartheid struggle in South Africa, the feminist movement, the gay rights movement, and the peace movement.

Maya Angelou's involvement in the Civil Rights Movement had a profound impact on her life and work. She witnessed the triumphs and tragedies of the movement, such as the Montgomery Bus Boycott, the March on Washington, the Selma to Montgomery March, the Birmingham Church Bombing, the assassination of Martin Luther King Jr., and the riots and rebellions that followed. She also experienced the joys and sorrows of her personal life, such as her love affairs, her marriages, her motherhood, her travels, her successes, and her challenges. She wrote about her experiences and reflections in her books and poems, such as I Know Why the Caged Bird Sings, The Heart of a Woman, And Still I Rise, and A Song Flung Up to Heaven. She shared her stories and insights with millions of people, and touched their hearts and minds.

Maya Angelou's involvement in the Civil Rights Movement was a testament to her passion and commitment. She believed in the power and potential of all people, especially Black people, women, and the oppressed. She spoke out against injustice and inequality, and stood up for freedom and dignity. She lived with courage and grace, and inspired others to do the same.

- Advocacy for equality and justice

Maya was a girl who cared about the world. She saw how people were treated differently and unfairly because of their skin color, their gender, their religion, or their background. She felt angry and sad, but she also felt hopeful and determined. She wanted to make the world a better place for everyone.

Maya learned from her grandmother, who taught her to respect herself and others, and to have faith in God. She learned from her mother, who taught her to be independent and adventurous, and to pursue her dreams. She learned from her brother, who taught her to be loyal and protective, and to have fun. She learned from her friends, who taught her to be supportive and compassionate, and to enjoy life.

Maya also learned from the people she admired and followed, who taught her to be courageous and active, and to fight for what is right. She learned from Martin Luther King Jr., who led the peaceful protests and campaigns for civil rights. She learned from Malcolm X, who advocated for Black empowerment and self-defense. She learned from

James Baldwin, who exposed the realities and complexities of racism in America. She learned from Nelson Mandela, who resisted the apartheid regime in South Africa. She learned from Gloria Steinem, who championed the feminist movement. She learned from many other activists, artists, and leaders who worked for social justice and human rights.

Maya decided to join them and to use her talents and skills to make a difference. She used her voice and her words to speak out against injustice and inequality, and to inspire and empower others. She used her actions and her deeds to stand up for freedom and dignity, and to support and help others. She used her stories and her poems to share her experiences and reflections, and to connect and educate others.

Maya was involved in many causes, actions, and moments that showed her dedication to equality and justice. She organized a cabaret for freedom to raise money for the Southern Christian Leadership Conference (SCLC) in 1959[^1^][1]. She served as the northern coordinator for the SCLC in 1960[^1^][1]. She joined Malcolm X in

33

planning for an Organization of Afro-American Unity in 1964[^2^][2]. She marched with Gloria Steinem and other women in the Women's Strike for Equality in 1970[^3^][3]. She recited her poem "On the Pulse of Morning" at the inauguration of President Bill Clinton in 1993. She also supported many other causes and movements, such as the anti-apartheid struggle in South Africa, the gay rights movement, and the peace movement.

Maya's advocacy for equality and justice had a profound impact on the world. She challenged the norms and conventions of society, and created new ways of thinking and acting. She reflected the realities and experiences of marginalized groups, and gave them a voice and a platform. She addressed the issues and problems of the times, and advocated for change and action. She inspired and influenced many other people, especially women and Black people, who found hope and courage in her words, and followed her example and vision. She educated and enlightened many people, who learned from her wisdom and insights, and connected with her stories and emotions. She motivated and empowered many people, who found strength and confidence in her words, and pursued their passions and goals.

7. Traveling the World
- Maya Angelou's global experiences

Maya was a girl who loved to travel. She was curious and adventurous, and she wanted to see and learn from the world. She believed that traveling was a way of expanding her mind and heart, and of discovering herself and others.

Maya began her travels when she was a teenager. She moved from Arkansas to California with her mother and brother, and experienced a different culture and lifestyle. She also traveled to Mexico with her father, and learned to drive a car and speak Spanish. She later moved to New York, where she met many artists and activists who inspired her to pursue her passions.

Maya continued her travels as an adult. She accepted a job as a dancer and singer in a touring production of Porgy and Bess, and visited 22 countries in Europe and Africa[^1^][1]. She was amazed by the diversity and beauty of the people and places she saw, and she also witnessed the effects of colonialism and racism. She decided to stay in Africa, and lived in Egypt and Ghana for several years[^2^][2]. She worked as a journalist, a teacher, and an editor, and met many influential figures, such as Malcolm X, Kwame Nkrumah, and W.E.B. Du Bois. She also found a home and a community among the African people, and learned about her roots and heritage.

Maya resumed her travels after returning to the US. She visited many countries in Asia, Europe, and Latin America, and learned about their cultures, histories, and struggles. She also participated in various events and causes, such as the inauguration of President Bill Clinton, the United Nations' 50th anniversary, and the anti-apartheid movement in South Africa[^3^][3]. She also received many honors and awards, such as the National Medal of Arts, the Presidential Medal of Freedom, and several honorary degrees.

Maya's travels had a profound impact on her work. She wrote about her experiences and observations in her books and poems, such as All God's Children Need Traveling Shoes, A Song Flung Up to Heaven, and On the Pulse of Morning. She shared her stories and insights with millions of people, and touched their hearts and minds. She also celebrated the diversity and potential of humanity, and the beauty and fragility of nature. She urged everyone to embrace and respect each other, and to work together for a better world.

- Cultural influences on her work

Maya was a girl who loved to learn. She was curious and open-minded, and she wanted to know and understand the world. She believed that learning was a way of growing and connecting, and of discovering herself and others.

Maya learned from many cultures and traditions, both in the US and abroad. She learned from the African-American culture, which was her heritage and identity. She learned from the stories and songs of her ancestors, who endured slavery and oppression, but also created art and resistance. She learned from the language and rhythms of the Black vernacular, which was rich and expressive, and which she used in her writing and speaking. She learned from the values and beliefs of the Black community, which was supportive and resilient, and which she celebrated and honored.

Maya also learned from other cultures and traditions, which she encountered through her travels and interactions. She learned from the African culture, which was her origin and connection. She learned from the history and politics of the African continent, which was diverse and complex, and which she witnessed and reported. She learned from the customs and practices of the African people, which were varied and colorful, and which she adopted and respected. She learned from the spirituality and philosophy of the African worldview, which was holistic and profound, and which she embraced and shared.

Maya learned from many other cultures and traditions, such as the Mexican, the Egyptian, the Ghanaian, the Chinese, the Indian, the French, and the Native American. She learned from their literature and art, their religion and science, their food and music, their wisdom and humor. She learned from their similarities and differences, their strengths and weaknesses, their joys and sorrows. She learned from their humanity and diversity, and she appreciated and valued them.

8. Leaving a Lasting Legacy
- Impact on literature and society

Maya was a girl who loved to write. She had a gift for words, and she used them to tell her stories and to share her views. She wrote about her life and the world around her, using her words to inspire and empower others. She was one of the most influential writers in American literature and culture, and her works have a lasting impact on readers of all ages and backgrounds.

Maya's works influenced the literary landscape in many ways. She challenged the norms and conventions of writing, and created new forms and styles of expression. She wrote in different genres and formats, such as autobiography, poetry, fiction, drama, and essays. She wrote in a voice that was authentic, honest, and expressive, and that captured the emotions and experiences of her characters and herself. She wrote in a language that was rich and musical, and that blended the Black vernacular with the literary tradition. She wrote with a purpose and a message, and that addressed the issues and problems of her time and beyond.

Maya's works contributed to societal conversations in many ways. She reflected the realities and experiences of marginalized groups, especially Black women, and gave them a voice and a platform. She addressed the issues and problems of the times, such as racism, sexism, violence, and injustice, and advocated for change and action. She inspired and influenced many other writers and artists, both in the US and abroad, who followed her example and vision. She educated and enlightened many readers and audiences, who learned from her wisdom and insights, and connected with her stories and emotions. She motivated and empowered many people, especially women and people of color, who found hope and courage in her words, and followed their dreams and passions.

Maya's works had a profound impact on literature and society, because they:

- Sparked change: Maya's works helped to change the literary and social landscape, by opening up new ways of writing and talking about race, gender, and trauma. Her works also helped to change the political and cultural landscape, by supporting and participating in various movements and causes, such as the Civil Rights Movement, the Women's Movement, and the Anti-Apartheid Movement[^1^][1] [^2^][2].

- Inspired individuals: Maya's works inspired many individuals, both famous and ordinary, who admired and respected her as a writer and a person. Some examples are Oprah Winfrey, who considered Maya as her mentor and friend, and who credited her for helping her overcome her own childhood trauma[^3^][3]; Barack Obama, who awarded Maya the Presidential Medal of Freedom, the highest civilian honor in the US, and who praised her for lifting the nation with her words; and Nelson Mandela, who recited Maya's poem "Still I Rise" at his presidential inauguration in South Africa, and who thanked her for her support and solidarity.

- Recognition and honors received

She was one of the most influential writers in American literature and culture, and she received many recognition and honors for her exceptional contributions.

Maya's recognition and honors came from many sources and fields. She received recognition and honors from universities, literary organizations, government agencies, and special interest groups. She received recognition and honors for her books, poems, speeches, and albums. She received recognition and honors for her achievements, contributions, and legacy.

Some of Maya's recognition and honors are:

- Pulitzer Prize nomination: This is one of the most prestigious awards in journalism and literature, and it recognizes excellence and originality in various categories. Maya was nominated for the Pulitzer Prize in 1972 for her first book of poetry, Just Give Me a Cool Drink of Water 'fore I Diiie[^1^][1]. This book showcased her skill and diversity as a poet, and it established her as a prominent voice in American literature.

- Tony Award nomination: This is one of the most prestigious awards in theater, and it recognizes excellence and achievement in various categories. Maya was nominated for the Tony Award in 1973 for her role in the Broadway play Look Away[^2^][2]. This play was based on the life of Mary Todd Lincoln, the wife of President Abraham Lincoln, and it explored the themes of mental illness, racism, and feminism.

- National Medal of Arts: This is the highest award given by the US government to artists and arts patrons, and it recognizes their outstanding contributions to the excellence, growth, and availability of the arts in the US. Maya was awarded the National Medal of Arts in 2000 by President Bill Clinton[^3^][3]. He praised her for lifting the nation with her words, and for being a role model and a leader for many people.

- Presidential Medal of Freedom: This is the highest civilian honor given by the US government, and it recognizes individuals who have made significant contributions to the security, peace, or national interests of the US, or to the world. Maya was awarded the Presidential

Medal of Freedom in 2010 by President Barack Obama. He praised her for her courage and grace, and for being a warrior for equality and justice.

- More than 50 honorary degrees: These are degrees conferred by universities to individuals who have distinguished themselves in various fields or causes, without requiring them to complete the usual academic requirements. Maya received more than 50 honorary degrees from various universities, such as Harvard, Yale, Princeton, and Oxford. She was honored for her achievements and contributions in literature, arts, education, civil rights, and human rights.

Maya's recognition and honors had a profound impact on her and the world. They validated and celebrated her work and worth, and they encouraged and motivated her to continue her passions and goals. They also influenced and inspired many other people, who admired and respected her as a writer and a person. They also contributed to the broader literary and cultural landscape, by opening up new ways of writing and talking about race, gender, and trauma, and by supporting and participating in various movements and causes, such as the Civil Rights Movement, the Women's Movement, and the Anti-Apartheid Movement.

9. Maya Angelou's Wisdom
- Inspirational quotes and life lessons for kids

She wrote many books and poems that taught us about life and the world. She also said many things that inspired us and made us think. Here are some of her quotes and what they mean:

- "I've learned that people will forget what you said, people will forget what you did, but people will never forget how you made them feel."[^1^][1]

This means that words and actions are important, but feelings are more important. How you treat others and how they treat you can make a big difference in your life. You should always try to be kind and respectful to others, and to make them feel good. You should also surround yourself with people who make you feel good, and who appreciate you for who you are.

- "You may not control all the events that happen to you, but you can decide not to be reduced by them."[^2^][2]

This means that life can be hard and unpredictable, and sometimes things happen that you don't like or expect. You can't always change what happens to you, but you can always change how you react to it. You can choose to be positive and hopeful, and to learn from your challenges. You can also choose to be strong and confident, and not to let your problems make you feel less than you are.

- "Do the best you can until you know better. Then when you know better, do better."[^3^][3]

This means that you should always try your best in everything you do, and be proud of your efforts. But you should also always try to learn new things and improve yourself. When you learn something new or realize something different, you should use that knowledge or understanding to do better next time. You should also admit your mistakes and apologize when you are wrong.

- "Nothing will work unless you do."

This means that you have to work hard to achieve your goals and dreams. You can't just wish for something or wait for someone else to do it for you. You have to take action and do your part. You have to be responsible and disciplined, and not give up easily. You also have to be creative and resourceful, and find ways to overcome obstacles.

- "When you learn, teach. When you get, give."

This means that you should share your knowledge and your resources with others. You should not keep everything to yourself, or be selfish or greedy. You should help others learn and grow, and you should also learn from others. You should also give back to your community and to the world, and be generous and grateful. You should also appreciate what you have, and not take anything for granted.

These are some of the life lessons that Maya Angelou taught us with her quotes. She was a remarkable woman, and a phenomenal teacher. She taught us how to use our words and actions to create beauty and meaning, to overcome adversity and injustice, to celebrate life and humanity, and to rise and soar.

- *Reflection on her teachings*

One of the people who learned from Maya Angelou was a young girl named Aisha. Aisha loved to read and write, and she dreamed of becoming a writer someday. She admired Maya Angelou, and she read her books and poems whenever she could. She also watched her videos and listened to her speeches online. She felt a connection with Maya Angelou, and she wanted to be like her.

Aisha learned many things from Maya Angelou, but there were three teachings that stood out for her. These were:

- "You may not control all the events that happen to you, but you can decide not to be reduced by them."[^1^][1]

Aisha learned that life can be hard and unpredictable, and sometimes things happen that are not fair or nice. She learned that she can't always change what happens to her, but she can always change how she reacts to it. She learned to be positive and hopeful, and to learn from her challenges. She learned to be strong and confident, and not to let her problems make her feel less than she is.

- "Do the best you can until you know better. Then when you know better, do better."

Aisha learned that she should always try her best in everything she does, and be proud of her efforts. But she also learned that she should always try to learn new things and improve herself. She learned that when she learns something new or realizes something different, she should use that knowledge or understanding to do better next time. She learned to admit her mistakes and apologize when she is wrong.

- "When you learn, teach. When you get, give."[^3^][3]

Aisha learned that she should share her knowledge and her resources with others. She learned that she should not keep everything to herself, or be selfish or greedy. She learned to help others learn and grow, and to also learn from others. She learned to give back to her community and to the world, and to be generous and grateful. She learned to appreciate what she has, and not take anything for granted.

Aisha applied these teachings in her own life, and she saw the results. She became a better student, a better friend, a better daughter, and a better person. She also became a better writer, and she wrote stories and poems that reflected her life and values. She shared her stories and poems with others, and they liked them. She also entered a writing contest, and she won a prize. She was very happy and proud.

Aisha thanked Maya Angelou for her teachings, and she wrote her a letter. She told her how much she admired and respected her, and how much she learned from her. She also told her how her teachings helped her achieve her dreams and overcome her challenges. She also told her how she wanted to continue learning and growing, and to follow her example and vision.

Maya Angelou received Aisha's letter, and she was very touched and pleased. She wrote back to Aisha, and she congratulated her on her prize and her achievements. She also encouraged her to keep writing and reading, and to keep following her dreams and passions. She also told her that she was proud of her, and that she loved her.

10. Fun Facts and Trivia

- Engaging tidbits about Maya Angelou's life

She had a very interesting and adventurous life, full of surprises and discoveries. Here are some of the captivating and engaging tidbits about her life that you might not know:

- She was a dancer and a singer before she became a writer. She performed in a touring production of Porgy and Bess, and visited 22 countries in Europe and Africa[1]. She also recorded a calypso album in 1957, and appeared in an off-Broadway musical called Calypso Heat Wave[2].

- She was the first Black woman to conduct a cable car in San Francisco. She was 16 years old when she applied for the job, and she lied about her age to get it. She said she loved the uniforms and the hats of the cable car conductors, and she wanted to wear them[3].

- She spoke six languages: English, French, Spanish, Hebrew, Italian, and Fante (a dialect of Akan native to Ghana). She learned them from her travels and interactions with different people and cultures. She also wrote some of her books in other languages, such as All God's Children Need Traveling Shoes, which she wrote in French.

- She was a close friend of Oprah Winfrey, the famous TV host and billionaire. They met in 1970, when Oprah was a young reporter and interviewed Maya for a show. They became like mother and daughter, and Maya gave Oprah many advice and gifts. One of the gifts was a quilt that belonged to Maya's grandmother, and Oprah said it was one of her most cherished possessions.

- She had a line of Hallmark greeting cards with her own quotes and poems. She started the collaboration with Hallmark in 2002, and she said she wanted to reach more people with her words. She said she liked the idea of people sending cards to each other, and she hoped her cards would make them feel good.

These are some of the tidbits about Maya Angelou's life that show her unique character and personality. She was a remarkable woman, and a phenomenal storyteller. She taught us how to use our words and actions to create beauty and meaning, to overcome adversity and injustice, to celebrate life and humanity, and to rise and soar.

- Interesting anecdotes for young readers

- When she was a little girl, she loved to read books and poems. She read everything she could find, from fairy tales to Shakespeare. She also memorized many poems, and recited them to herself and to others. She said that reading and reciting poems helped her overcome her fear of speaking, and gave her confidence and joy.

- When she was a teenager, she decided to become a cable car conductor in San Francisco. She thought it was a fun and exciting job, and she liked the uniforms and the hats. But when she went to apply for the job, they refused to give her an application form, because she was Black and a girl. She did not give up, and she went to the office every day for two weeks, until they finally gave her a chance. She became the first Black woman to do that job, and she was very proud of it.

- When she was a young woman, she traveled around the world as a dancer and a singer. She performed in a musical called Porgy and Bess, and visited 22 countries in Europe and Africa[1]. She saw many beautiful and amazing things, and she also learned about the cultures and histories of the people she met. She also learned to speak six languages: English, French, Spanish, Hebrew, Italian, and Fante (a dialect of Akan native to Ghana).

- When she was in her twenties, she lived in Egypt and Ghana for several years. She worked as a journalist, a teacher, and an editor, and she wrote about the events and issues that were happening in Africa. She also met many famous and influential people, such as Malcolm X, Kwame Nkrumah, and W.E.B. Du Bois. She also found a home and a community among the African people, and she felt a connection with her roots and heritage.

- When she was in her forties, she wrote her first book, I Know Why the Caged Bird Sings. It was an autobiography, which means a story of her own life. She wrote about her childhood and adolescence, and the things that happened to her, both good and bad. She wrote with honesty and courage, and she shared her feelings and thoughts. Her book was a huge success, and it made her famous and respected as a writer.

These are some of the stories from Maya Angelou's life that show her character and personality. She was a remarkable woman, and a phenomenal storyteller. She taught us how to use our words and actions to create beauty and meaning, to overcome adversity and injustice, to celebrate life and humanity, and to rise and soar.

11. Timeline of Maya Angelou's Life
- *Chronological overview from birth to legacy*

- 1928: Maya Angelou is born on April 4 in St. Louis, Missouri. Her real name is Marguerite Annie Johnson. Her parents are Bailey Johnson, a doorman, and Vivian Johnson, a nurse.

- 1931: Maya and her older brother, Bailey Jr, are sent by their parents to live with their grandmother, Annie Henderson, in Stamps, Arkansas. They experience racism and poverty in the rural South

- 1935: Maya and Bailey return to their mother in St. Louis. Maya is raped by her mother's boyfriend, Freeman, when she is seven years old. She tells her brother, who tells the rest of the family. Freeman is arrested, tried, and released. He is later found dead, presumably killed by Maya's uncles. Maya feels guilty and stops speaking for five years, thinking that her words have caused his death.

- 1937: Maya meets Mrs. Bertha Flowers, a Black woman who introduces her to books and poetry. She helps Maya to overcome her trauma and find her voice again.

- 1940: Maya moves with her mother to San Francisco, California. She attends George Washington High School and studies dance and drama at the California Labor School.

- 1942: Maya becomes the first Black woman to work as a cable car conductor in San Francisco. She lies about her age to get the job, which she likes because of the uniforms and hats.

- 1944: Maya graduates from high school and gives birth to her son, Clyde, later renamed Guy Johnson. The father is her high school boyfriend, Bailey Johnson Jr.

- 1945: Maya marries Tosh Angelos, a Greek sailor and musician. They divorce after three years of marriage.

- 1951: Maya marries Anastasios Angelopulos, a Greek electrician and aspiring writer. They divorce after eight years of marriage.

- 1954: Maya joins a touring production of Porgy and Bess, a musical by George Gershwin. She visits 22 countries in Europe and Africa as a dancer and singer.

- 1957: Maya records a calypso album called Miss Calypso and appears in an off-Broadway musical called Calypso Heat Wave.

- 1958: Maya moves to New York and joins the Harlem Writers Guild, a group of Black writers and activists. She meets John Oliver Killens, James Baldwin, Langston Hughes, and other influential figures in the literary and cultural scene.

- 1959: Maya meets Martin Luther King Jr., the leader of the Southern Christian Leadership Conference (SCLC), a civil rights organization. She becomes the northern coordinator of the SCLC and organizes a cabaret for freedom to raise funds for the group.

- 1960: Maya performs in Jean Genet's play The Blacks, along with Cicely Tyson, James Earl Jones, and other Black actors. The play is a commentary on racism and colonialism.

- 1961: Maya meets Malcolm X, the leader of the Nation of Islam, a Black nationalist and religious group. She is impressed by his charisma and intelligence.

- 1962: Maya moves to Cairo, Egypt, with her son and her boyfriend, Vusumzi Make, a South African anti-apartheid activist. She works as an editor for The Arab Observer, an English-language weekly newspaper.

- 1964: Maya returns to the US and rejoins Malcolm X, who has left the Nation of Islam and founded the

Organization of Afro-American Unity (OAAU), a secular and pan-Africanist group. She helps him to plan for a trip to Africa to build alliances with African leaders.

- 1965: Malcolm X is assassinated on February 21 in New York. Maya is devastated by his death and decides to move to Ghana with her son, who has been injured in a car accident. She works as a lecturer, a journalist, and an editor at the University of Ghana. She meets Kwame Nkrumah, the president of Ghana, and W.E.B. Du Bois, the founder of the NAACP, who dies in Ghana in August.

- 1968: Martin Luther King Jr. is assassinated on April 4, Maya's 40th birthday, in Memphis, Tennessee. Maya is shocked and saddened by his death, and decides to return to the US. She is encouraged by James Baldwin and Robert Loomis, an editor at Random House, to write her autobiography.

- 1969: Maya publishes her first book, I Know Why the Caged Bird Sings, which covers her life from age three to 16. The book is a critical and commercial success, and it is nominated for the National Book Award. It is also one of the first books by a Black woman to gain widespread recognition and acclaim.

- 1970: Maya publishes her first poetry collection, Just Give Me a Cool Drink of Water 'fore I Diiie, which is nominated for the Pulitzer Prize. She also writes the screenplay and the musical score for the film Georgia, Georgia, becoming the first Black woman to do so.

- 1972: Maya writes the screenplay and the musical score for the film adaptation of her book I Know Why the Caged Bird Sings, which is broadcast on CBS. She also writes the original script for the film All Day Long, which is later revised and released as Black Girl.

- 1973: Maya marries Paul du Feu, a British carpenter and writer. They divorce in 1981.

- 1974: Maya publishes her second autobiography, Gather Together in My Name, which covers her life from age 17 to 19. She also publishes her second poetry collection, Oh Pray My Wings Are Gonna Fit Me Well.

- 1975: Maya publishes her third autobiography, Singin' and Swingin' and Gettin' Merry Like Christmas, which covers her life from age 21 to 27. She also publishes her third poetry collection, And Still I Rise, which includes her famous poem "Still I Rise".

- 1976: Maya publishes her fourth autobiography, The Heart of a Woman, which covers her life from age 28 to 37.

She also publishes her fourth poetry collection, Shaker, Why Don't You Sing?.

- 1977: Maya appears in the television mini-series Roots, based on the book by Alex Haley. She plays Kunta Kinte's grandmother, Nyo Boto.

- 1979: Maya receives an Emmy nomination for her role in Roots. She also narrates the documentary I Shall Not Be Moved, which chronicles the history of the civil rights movement.

- 1981: Maya moves to Winston-Salem, North Carolina, and becomes a professor of American studies at Wake Forest University. She also publishes her fifth autobiography, All God's Children Need Traveling Shoes, which covers her life from age 33 to 39.

- 1983: Maya recites her poem "On the Pulse of Morning" at the inauguration of President Bill Clinton. She is the first poet to do so since Robert Frost in 1961, and the first African American and woman to do so. She also receives a Grammy Award for the audio recording of the poem.

- 1986: Maya directs her first feature film, Down in the Delta, starring Alfre Woodard and Wesley Snipes. The film is about a drug-addicted woman who reconnects with her family and heritage in the rural South.

- 1993: Maya publishes her sixth autobiography, A Song Flung Up to Heaven, which covers her life from age 40 to 41. She also publishes her fifth poetry collection, I Shall Not Be Moved

- 1994: Maya receives the Spingarn Medal from the NAACP, the highest honor given by the organization. She also receives three more Grammy Awards for the audio recordings of her poems and books.

- 1995: Maya publishes her sixth poetry collection, Phenomenal Woman, which includes four poems celebrating women's strength and beauty.

- 1998: Maya publishes her first children's book, My Painted House, My Friendly Chicken, and Me, which is based on her visit to a Ndebele village in South Africa. She also publishes her seventh poetry collection, A Brave and Startling Truth, which includes the poem she wrote for the 50th anniversary of the United Nations.

- 2000: Maya receives the National Medal of Arts from President Bill Clinton, the highest award given by the US government to artists and arts patrons. She also publishes her second children's book, Kofi and His Magic, which is based on her visit to a Ghanaian village.

- 2002: Maya publishes her seventh autobiography, Mom & Me & Mom, which focuses on her relationship with her mother. She also publishes her eighth poetry collection, Amazing Peace, which includes the poem she wrote for the lighting of the National Christmas Tree at the White House.

- 2008: Maya supports Barack Obama's presidential campaign and recites her poem "His Day Is Done" at his inauguration. She also receives the Lincoln Medal from President Obama, an award given to individuals who exemplify the legacy and

12. Activities and Exercises
- Interactive content to engage young readers

Welcome to Maya Angelou's World, a place where you can learn about the amazing life and work of one of the most influential writers and activists in history. You will discover how she overcame many challenges and achieved many dreams, and how she used her words and actions to inspire and empower others. You will also have the chance to explore, reflect, and express yourself, and to create your own stories and poems.

Are you ready to begin? Let's go!

Chapter 1: Growing Up

Maya Angelou was born on April 4, 1928, in St. Louis, Missouri. Her real name was Marguerite Annie Johnson, but her brother Bailey called her Maya, which means "my sister" in Arabic. Her parents were Bailey Johnson, a doorman, and Vivian Johnson, a nurse. They divorced when Maya was three years old, and sent her and Bailey to live with their grandmother, Annie Henderson, in Stamps, Arkansas.

Stamps was a small town in the rural South, where Maya and Bailey faced racism and poverty every day. They also faced violence and abuse, especially when they returned to their mother in St. Louis, and Maya was raped by her mother's boyfriend, Freeman, when she was seven years old. She told her brother, who told the rest of the family. Freeman was arrested, tried, and released. He was later found dead, presumably killed by Maya's uncles. Maya felt guilty and stopped speaking for five years, thinking that her words had caused his death.

But Maya did not give up on her dreams. She found solace in books and poetry, and learned from the wisdom of great writers and thinkers. She also found mentors and friends who encouraged her to express herself and find her voice. She discovered that she had a gift for storytelling and singing, and that she could use her words to inspire and empower others.

Activity 1: Reading and Reciting Poems

Maya loved to read and recite poems. She said that reading and reciting poems helped her overcome her fear of speaking, and gave her confidence and joy. She learned many poems by heart, and recited them to herself and to others.

In this activity, you will read and recite some of the poems that Maya loved. You will also learn about the poets who wrote them, and the themes and messages they convey.

Here are some of the poems that Maya loved:

- "Invictus" by William Ernest Henley
- "Sympathy" by Paul Laurence Dunbar
- "Dreams" by Langston Hughes
- "Still I Rise" by Maya Angelou

Choose one of the poems and read it aloud. Pay attention to the words, the sounds, the rhythms, and the emotions. Try to understand what the poem means, and how it relates to Maya's life and yours.

Then, answer these questions:

- What is the title of the poem and who is the poet?
- What is the main theme or message of the poem?
- How does the poem make you feel?
- How does the poem relate to Maya's life and yours?

Write your answers in a paragraph, and share them with a friend or a family member.

Activity 2: Writing Your Own Poem

Maya was not only a reader and a reciter of poems, but also a writer of poems. She wrote many poems that reflected her life and values. She wrote about love, pain, hope, and courage. She wrote about herself, her people, her country, and her planet.

In this activity, you will write your own poem. You will use your imagination and creativity, and express your feelings and thoughts. You will also use some of the poetic devices that Maya used, such as imagery, metaphor, rhyme, and repetition.

Here are some of the steps to write your own poem:

- Choose a topic or a theme that you want to write about. It can be something that you care about, something that you wonder about, something that you wish for, or something that you feel.
- Think of some words or phrases that describe your topic or theme. Use your senses, your emotions, your memories, or your imagination. Write them down on a piece of paper or a notebook.
- Arrange your words or phrases into lines and stanzas. A line is a single row of words, and a stanza is a group of lines. You can have as many lines and stanzas as you want, but try to make them balanced and consistent. You can also use punctuation and capitalization to create pauses and emphasis.

- Add some poetic devices to make your poem more interesting and memorable. You can use imagery, which is the use of words to create pictures in the reader's mind. You can use metaphor, which is the comparison of two things that are not alike. You can use rhyme, which is the repetition of sounds at the end of words. You can use repetition, which is the use of the same word or phrase more than once.

Here is an example of a poem that Maya wrote, using some of these poetic devices:

You may write me down in history
With your bitter, twisted lies,
You may tread me in the very dirt
But still, like dust, I'll rise.

This is the first stanza of her poem "Still I Rise", which is about her resilience and empowerment. She uses imagery, such as "write me down in history" and "tread me in the very dirt". She uses metaphor, such as "like dust, I'll rise".

She uses rhyme, such as "lies" and "rise". She uses repetition, such as "You may" and "I'll rise".

Now, write your own poem, using some of these poetic devices. Write it on a piece of paper or a notebook, and decorate it with colors and drawings. Then, read it aloud, and share it with a friend or a family member. Enjoy your poem, and be proud of your work.

Chapter 2: Traveling the World

Maya Angelou loved to travel. She was curious and adventurous, and she wanted to see and learn from the world. She believed that traveling was a way of expanding her mind and heart, and of discovering herself and others.

Maya began her travels when she was a teenager. She moved from Arkansas to California with her mother and brother, and experienced a different culture and lifestyle. She also traveled to Mexico with her father, and learned to drive a car and speak Spanish.

Maya continued her travels as an adult. She accepted a job as a dancer and singer in a touring production of Porgy and Bess, and visited 22 countries in Europe and Africa. She was amazed by the diversity and beauty of the people and places she saw, and she also witnessed the effects of colonialism and racism. She decided to stay in Africa, and lived in Egypt and Ghana for several years. She worked as a journalist, a teacher, and an editor, and met many influential figures, such as Malcolm X, Kwame Nkrumah, and W.E.B. Du Bois. She also found a home and a community among the African people, and learned about her roots and heritage.

Maya resumed her travels after returning to the US. She visited many countries in Asia, Europe, and Latin America, and learned about their cultures, histories, and struggles. She also participated in various events and causes, such as the inauguration of President Bill Clinton, the United Nations' 50th anniversary, and the anti-apartheid movement in South Africa.

Activity 1: Mapping Maya's Travels

Maya traveled to many places around the world, and each place had a special meaning and impact on her life and work. She wrote about her travels and observations in her books and poems, and shared them with millions of people.

In this activity, you will map Maya's travels, and learn about the places she visited and the things she did. You will also learn about the geography and the culture of each place, and how they relate to Maya's story and yours.

Here are some of the places that Maya visited:

- San Francisco, California, USA
- Mexico City, Mexico
- New York, New York, USA
- Paris, France
- Rome, Italy
- Cairo, Egypt
- Accra, Ghana

- Beijing, China
- Delhi, India
- Johannesburg, South Africa
- Washington, DC, USA

Choose one of the places and find it on a map. You can use a paper map, a globe, or an online map. Pay attention to the location, the shape, the size, and the neighbors of the place. Try to answer these questions:

- What continent is the place on?
- What country is the place in?
- What is the capital of the country?
- What are the neighboring countries or states?
- What are the main physical features of the place, such as mountains, rivers, lakes, or oceans?

Then, research some information about the place, such as the history, the culture, the people, and the attractions. You can use books, magazines, websites, or other sources. Try to answer these questions:

- What is the population of the place?

- What are the main languages spoken in the place?

- What are the main religions practiced in the place?

- What are the main foods eaten in the place?

- What are the main festivals or celebrations in the place?

Finally, find out what Maya did in the place, and how it affected her life and work. You can use her books, poems, interviews, or other sources. Try to answer these questions:

- When and why did Maya visit the place?

- What did Maya do or see in the place?

- Who did Maya meet or work with in the place?

- What did Maya do or see in the place?

- How did the place affect her life and work?

Here are some examples of the answers for each place:

- San Francisco, California, USA

77

- Maya visited San Francisco in 1940, when she moved there with her mother and brother. She also returned there several times later in her life.

- Maya did many things in San Francisco, such as working as a cable car conductor, studying dance and drama, becoming a calypso singer, and writing her first book.

- Maya saw many things in San Francisco, such as the Golden Gate Bridge, the cable cars, the Chinatown, and the diverse and vibrant culture.

- San Francisco affected Maya's life and work in many ways, such as giving her opportunities and challenges, exposing her to different arts and people, and inspiring her creativity and confidence.

- Mexico City, Mexico

- Maya visited Mexico City in 1944, when she traveled there with her father for a month.

- Maya did many things in Mexico City, such as learning to drive a car, speaking Spanish, and experiencing the Mexican culture and cuisine.

- Maya saw many things in Mexico City, such as the Zocalo, the Cathedral, the National Palace, and the Frida Kahlo Museum.

- Mexico City affected Maya's life and work in many ways, such as giving her independence and adventure, exposing her to a different language and history, and inspiring her curiosity and courage.

- New York, New York, USA

- Maya visited New York in 1958, when she moved there to pursue her writing career. She also returned there several times later in her life.

- Maya did many things in New York, such as joining the Harlem Writers Guild, performing in The Blacks, writing for The Arab Observer, and publishing her first book of poetry.

- Maya saw many things in New York, such as the Statue of Liberty, the Empire State Building, the Broadway, and the Harlem Renaissance.

- New York affected Maya's life and work in many ways, such as giving her ambition and recognition, exposing her to different writers and activists, and inspiring her expression and empowerment.

- Paris, France

- Maya visited Paris in 1954, when she performed there with the Porgy and Bess cast. She also returned there several times later in her life.

- Maya did many things in Paris, such as singing and dancing, visiting the Louvre, meeting James Baldwin, and writing her screenplay for Georgia, Georgia.

- Maya saw many things in Paris, such as the Eiffel Tower, the Notre Dame, the Champs-Elysees, and the French culture and fashion.

- Paris affected Maya's life and work in many ways, such as giving her elegance and sophistication, exposing her to different arts and people, and inspiring her beauty and grace.

- Rome, Italy

- Maya visited Rome in 1954, when she performed there with the Porgy and Bess cast. She also returned there several times later in her life.

- Maya did many things in Rome, such as singing and dancing, visiting the Colosseum, meeting Langston Hughes, and writing her musical score for All Day Long.

- Maya saw many things in Rome, such as the Vatican, the Trevi Fountain, the Roman Forum, and the Italian culture and cuisine.

- Rome affected Maya's life and work in many ways, such as giving her history and romance, exposing her to different arts and people, and inspiring her passion and creativity.

- Cairo, Egypt

- Maya visited Cairo in 1962, when she moved there with her son and her boyfriend, Vusumzi Make. She lived there for two years.

- Maya did many things in Cairo, such as working as an editor for The Arab Observer, learning Arabic, and participating in the African liberation movement.

- Maya saw many things in Cairo, such as the Pyramids, the Nile, the Sphinx, and the Egyptian culture and politics.

- Cairo affected Maya's life and work in many ways, such as giving her knowledge and perspective, exposing her to a different language and history, and inspiring her curiosity and courage.

- Accra, Ghana

- Maya visited Accra in 1964, when she moved there with her son, who had been injured in a car accident. She lived there for four years.

- Maya did many things in Accra, such as working as a lecturer, a journalist, and an editor, meeting Malcolm X, Kwame Nkrumah, and W.E.B. Du Bois, and finding a home and a community among the African people.

- Maya saw many things in Accra, such as the Independence Square, the National Museum, the Kwame

Nkrumah Mausoleum, and the Ghanaian culture and heritage.

- Accra affected Maya's life and work in many ways, such as giving her identity and connection, exposing her to a different language and history, and inspiring her wisdom and pride.

- Beijing, China

Maya did many things in Beijing, China. Here are some of them:

- She met and befriended many writers and artists from Africa and Asia, and learned about their cultures and perspectives. She also shared her own experiences and views, and participated in discussions and debates about literature, politics, and society.

- She visited many historical and cultural sites, such as the Forbidden City, the Great Wall, the Temple of Heaven, and the Summer Palace. She admired the architecture and the art, and learned about the history and the symbolism of each place.

- She experienced the everyday life and the customs of the Chinese people, such as eating dumplings, drinking tea, riding bicycles, and practicing tai chi. She also learned some words and phrases in Mandarin, and tried to communicate with the locals.

- She wrote some poems and essays inspired by her travels and observations, such as "A Brave and Startling Truth", which she wrote for the 50th anniversary of the United Nations in 1995. She also wrote a foreword for a book by a Chinese poet, Bei Dao, in 1997.

- Creative projects inspired by Maya Angelou's life

Maya Angelou was an amazing writer and a wonderful person. She had a very interesting and adventurous life, full of surprises and discoveries. She used her words and actions to create beauty and meaning, to overcome adversity and injustice, to celebrate life and humanity, and to rise and soar.

You can learn more about Maya Angelou and her work by doing some creative projects that will inspire you and challenge you. You can also express yourself and connect with the themes of her journey, such as resilience, creativity, and the pursuit of dreams. You can use different mediums, such as art, writing, or performance, to show your creativity and have fun.

Here are creative projects that you can do:

Project 1: Make a Collage of Maya Angelou's Life

A collage is a piece of art that is made by putting together different materials, such as paper, fabric, or photos, on a surface. You can make a collage of Maya Angelou's life, using images and words that represent her story and achievements.

You will need:

- A large piece of paper or cardboard
- Scissors

- Glue

- Magazines, newspapers, books, or printouts of images and words related to Maya Angelou

- Markers, crayons, or colored pencils

Here are the steps to make your collage:

- Cut out images and words from the magazines, newspapers, books, or printouts that relate to Maya Angelou's life. You can use images and words that show her childhood, her travels, her work, her awards, her friends, and her legacy. You can also use images and words that show her interests, her passions, her values, and her dreams.

- Arrange the images and words on the paper or cardboard in a way that tells a story or creates a pattern. You can make a timeline, a map, a portrait, or a mosaic. You can also make a theme, a symbol, a message, or a question.

- Glue the images and words on the paper or cardboard, and make sure they are secure and neat.

- Add some details and decorations with the markers, crayons, or colored pencils. You can draw borders, backgrounds, frames, or shapes. You can also write titles, captions, quotes, or poems.

- Display your collage in a place where you and others can see it and admire it.

Project 2: Write a Letter to Maya Angelou

A letter is a written message that is sent to someone. You can write a letter to Maya Angelou, telling her how much you admire and respect her, and how much you learned from her.

You will need:

- A piece of paper or a notebook
- A pen or a pencil
- An envelope and a stamp (optional)

Here are the steps to write your letter:

- Write the date and the salutation at the top of the paper or the notebook. The salutation is the way you greet someone, such as "Dear Maya Angelou," or "Hello Maya Angelou,"

- Write the body of the letter, which is the main part of your message. You can write about:

  - Who you are and why you are writing to her
  - What you like and admire about her and her work
  - What you learned and gained from reading her books and poems
  - How her words and actions inspired and influenced you
  - What questions or comments you have for her
  - What you wish or hope for her and yourself

- Write the closing and the signature at the bottom of the paper or the notebook. The closing is the way you say goodbye, such as "Sincerely," or "With love," The signature is your name or nickname.

- Fold the paper or the notebook and put it in the envelope. Write your address and Maya Angelou's address on the envelope. Put the stamp on the envelope. (You can find Maya Angelou's address online or in a book.)

- Mail your letter or keep it as a souvenir.

Project 3: Perform a Poem by Maya Angelou

A poem is a piece of writing that uses words to create images, sounds, rhythms, and emotions. You can perform a poem by Maya Angelou, using your voice and your body to express the meaning and the feeling of the poem.

You will need:

- A copy of a poem by Maya Angelou
- A microphone or a speaker (optional)
- A costume or a prop (optional)

Here are the steps to perform your poem:

- Choose a poem by Maya Angelou that you like and that you can relate to. You can find her poems online or in a book. Some of her famous poems are:

- "Still I Rise"

- "Phenomenal Woman"

- "Caged Bird"

- "On the Pulse of Morning"

- Read the poem aloud several times, and try to understand what the poem means and how it makes you feel. Pay attention to the words, the sounds, the rhythms, and the emotions. Try to memorize the poem or use the copy as a guide.

- Practice the poem in front of a mirror or a friend, and try to use your voice and your body to express the meaning and the feeling of the poem. You can use different tones, volumes, speeds, and pauses to create contrast and emphasis. You can also use gestures, movements, expressions, and poses to create images and emotions.

- Prepare for your performance by choosing a microphone or a speaker, if you want to make your voice louder or clearer. You can also choose a costume or a prop, if you want to make your performance more interesting or fun. You can wear something that matches the theme or the mood of the poem, or use something that represents the poem or yourself.

- Perform your poem in front of an audience, such as your family, your friends, your classmates, or your teacher. You can perform your poem at home, at school, or at a public place. You can also record your performance and share it online or with others. Enjoy your performance, and be proud of your work.

13. Conclusion

Maya Angelou taught us many things about life and the world, through her books, poems, speeches, and films. She taught us how to love, how to learn, how to grow, and how to live. She taught us how to use our words and actions to create beauty and meaning, to overcome adversity and injustice, to celebrate life and humanity, and to rise and soar.

Maya Angelou left a lasting legacy in literature and culture, and in the hearts and minds of millions of people. She left a legacy of courage and grace, of wisdom and compassion, of hope and joy. She left a legacy of stories and poems, of images and sounds, of emotions and messages. She left a legacy of humanity and diversity, of peace and justice, of freedom and dignity.

Maya Angelou was a remarkable woman, and a phenomenal achiever. She showed us what is possible when we follow our dreams and passions, and when we work hard and never give up. She also showed us what is important when we face difficulties and uncertainties, and when we help others and make a difference. She also showed us what is beautiful when we express ourselves and connect with others, and when we appreciate and respect the world and ourselves.

Maya Angelou was an inspiration and a guide, and she still is. She inspired and guided many people, both famous and ordinary, who admired and respected her as a writer and a person. She also inspired and guided us, and she still does. She inspired and guided us to learn and create, to overcome and achieve, to celebrate and love, and to rise and soar.

Maya Angelou was a star and a friend, and she still is. She was a star that shone brightly and warmly, and that made the world a better place. She was also a friend that spoke kindly and honestly, and that made us feel good. She was a star and a friend to us, and she still is. She is a star and a friend that we can look up to and talk to, and that we can remember and cherish.

Maya Angelou was a phenomenal woman, and she still is. She was a phenomenal woman who lived a phenomenal life, and who gave us phenomenal gifts. She is a phenomenal woman who lives in our hearts and minds, and who gives us phenomenal lessons. She is a phenomenal woman who we can admire and respect, and who we can thank and honor.

Thank you, Maya Angelou, for your phenomenal life and work. Thank you for your phenomenal legacy and inspiration. Thank you for your phenomenal words and actions. Thank you for being a phenomenal woman, and for being our phenomenal friend. We love you, Maya Angelou, and we always will.

Printed in Great Britain
by Amazon